I Am Not The Same Girl

I Am Not The Same Girl
RENEWED

Stacy Lattisaw Jackson

Believers Building Bridges
Fort Washington, Maryland

Cover design by Tamika L. Hayden, TLH Designs, Chicago, IL
Book design by Kingdom Living Publishing, Fort Washington, MD

For information about this book or to contact the author, write to:

Believers Building Bridges Company
P.O. Box 44330
Fort Washington, MD 20744

You may also send the author an email message at
stacy@stacylattisaw.net

Published by:

Believers Building Bridges Company
Fort Washington, MD

Printed in the United States of America.

ISBN 978-0-615-40774-6

First Edition: March 2011
10 9 8 7 6 5 4 3 2 1

Dedication

I dedicate this book to all of my fans who have supported me throughout the years. Almost 19 years ago, I came to a crossroad in my life and things began to change—not outwardly but inwardly. I had been in search of REAL peace for a long time; so I began to seek God to find out more about who HE is. Then I realized who I was and what HIS purpose was for me. For so long many have asked me, "Where have you been?" "What have you been doing?" "Why are you no longer singing R&B [Rhythm and Blues] music?" Well, after reading this book you will not only find out where I have been, but who I am today. *I AM NOT THE SAME GIRL: RENEWED.*

Table of Contents

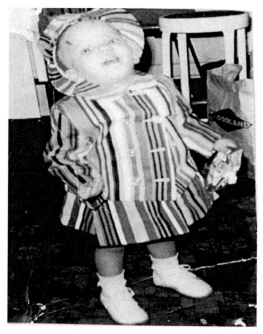
The author as a toddler

November 25, 1966, marked the beginning of a life that would endure stardom, pain, and then change.

Chapter 1

Before the Music

My early years took place in Southeast Washington, DC—the stomping grounds for my two sisters, brother, and me. Though growing up in Southeast was not necessarily the greatest of living conditions, we all adapted with time. Many would consider my family to be rather large compared to the average family nowadays. In our diminutive home, there lived my parents Saundra and Jerome Sr., my sisters Saundra and Sheila, my brother Jerome Jr., and I.

Saundra (nicknamed Pinky by our mother) was the oldest of the four of us. She was always extremely protective of her siblings. Everywhere we went Pinky would always stay close and ensure the safety of Jerome, Sheila, and me. Then there was my second oldest sister, Sheila. Ever since we were young, I couldn't tell you a time where Sheila was called selfish. As I always could remember, she had a very giving and generous spirit. In times of trouble at a young age (problems weren't severe at the time), I would go and talk to Sheila because of the comforting advice I knew she would give. The youngest of the children was my brother Jerome Jr. (whom we nicknamed Jerry). Out of all my family, I would have to say that Jerry and I are the most alike. We often share the same opinions on situations and feel the same way about everyday life scenarios. We were the closest, and there was no awkward conversing between the two of us. I could tell him anything and vice versa. In our early years, I spent the majority of my home time with him playing board games, watching cartoons, laughing, and just enjoying the carefree times of being children.

If I could explain my parents' characteristics in a sentence, I would say that they were protective, loving, caring, yet strict all at the same time. They are remarkable examples of what parents should be. I always looked at my mother as the woman I wanted to be even at the young age I was then. Sheila's selflessness was a trait that came from my mother. She never had a "me-first" attitude when it came to us. My mother thought about her family first in every situation and event that occurred. It was a blessing that she was able to be a stay-at-home mom because I believe that allowed her to always keep an eye on all of her children and help keep us on track at all times. She seemingly was involved in every decision my sisters, brother, and I made growing up. From anything as little as playmates to the bigger things down the road, she always had a significant input.

Well, at times it wasn't input; it was more like "the final decision" because she always made sure we did right. There were times when she wouldn't let me do certain things, which other kids did; that seemed perfectly fine by me. I used to get upset, but she obviously knew what was best for me. My dad was the hard worker of the family. He worked at the Government Printing Office for 36 long years, being committed to his job ever since I could remember. My father made a lot of sacrifices for us all, being the rock of the family, remaining strong and confident, keeping things together. Just as it was for my mother, family was always the top priority for him.

Being young had its many joys, but then came school. At five years old I started kindergarten. I attended Kimball Elementary School. In the beginning, I remember crying everyday and quite often, my mother would cry also from watching me cry, knowing that she would have to leave me in that state. I guess it was because I was so attached to her and I was so shy. Because we lived only two to three blocks from Kimball Elementary, my mother was able to walk me to school every morning. Walking those blocks to school seemed to be so short timed because of the mere fact that I didn't want to go. Yet with that bad feeling at the pit of my stomach, my mother still accompanied me every day, which was another sure sacrifice. One of the benefits of being so close to the school was that I was fortunate enough to come home for lunch every day.

My mother would walk to the school at the middle of the school day to take me home, feed me, and walk me back in time before class resumed. Though it was lunch time, my mother often made me pancakes, because that was one of my favorite foods to eat as a child. I was so convinced that my mother made the best pancakes in the world. As you can see, my mother was very concerned for the well being of all of us, even when it came to clothing. Though our finances weren't great, my mother took pride in dressing us by purchasing the finest clothes for my sisters, brother, and me. She always made sure that we were color coordinated from our tops to the shoes on our feet.

She set the foundation for my sisters and me and our daintiness by ensuring the importance of hygiene and being presentable at all times. Our hair was never undone even at that young age. My hair was often pressed with a hot comb. In my mind, my mother's time pressing my hair and fixing it up with ponytails and frontal bangs was sometimes in vain, because I would later go outside to play only to end up sweating until my hair turned back into a frizzy bush. However, she continued to do it with pride day in and day out.

Throughout kindergarten and first grade, I was a shy girl and stayed to myself. It wasn't until the second grade that I started to feel a little more comfortable with school and didn't dread going as I had before. Mrs. Carter, my second grade teacher, played a huge role in my changed feelings about school. She would be my favorite teacher of all my school years. I couldn't exactly figure out what it was about Mrs. Carter that made me feel so comfortable once I entered her classroom. She was always very gentle and patient with each student; she put forth ample time to make sure every student understood exactly what she was teaching, even though we were only second graders. Every morning in her class, she would go around the room to give out oatmeal cookies and milk for students who may have not had breakfast. Although I had breakfast every morning, I would still take them because I loved oatmeal cookies; and every morning on way to school, this would always give me something to look forward to. Both my mother and I were very fond of Mrs. Carter. That was an enjoyable year for me compared to some of my others.

While young, most children my age played with dolls and things of that nature. But for me, I always had an unusual interest in cash registers. I would always tell my mother that I wanted to be a cashier when I grew up; she would look at me and laugh. I owned different toy cash registers growing up. I loved pushing the buttons and hearing the sounds of opening and shutting the cash drawers. I would then cut up paper to make fake money to play "store" with my brother Jerry. As fast as I could play with toys, my parents would buy me new ones. Believe it or not, every day my father came home from work he would bring me something new. Whether it was a Barbie doll or something as little as a puzzle, he kept me running to the door every day at 6 o'clock p.m.

to welcome him home with a hug and a kiss and to see what he had for me. I have always been a daddy's girl. And I still am today.

After completing elementary school, I attended Sousa Junior High School. Because middle school was farther from home, my grandfather, Joseph Lattisaw, used to take me to school and pick me up every day. I remember some people used to say, "Wow, there is a yellow Cadillac out there." I do not remember where he lived back then, but he made that sacrifice every morning to take me to school; and wherever he was around 3 o'clock p.m., he would stop what he was doing to pick me up and take me back home. As I look back on it now, he didn't have to do that, but he did. I am so thankful because I have had great people in my life who have done selfless things for me. I count it a blessing. My grandfather is still living. He is 95 years old. I always tell him that he did something right because he is still living today and is doing quite well. I thank God for his life and the many ways he shows his love and support to us all. He now lives with my parents. There are two things that my grandfather loves to do: play cards and eat crabs. That keeps a smile on his face.

My dad's mother passed away when I was about six years old, so I really don't remember much about her. But I remember her pretty smile and her spirit. I wish that both of my grandmothers could have lived long enough to see my kids grow up, because I know they would have loved them. My parents often say that I remind them of my father's mom. I've been told that I have her smile and traits of her personality.

I remember someone told me a long time ago that she was a woman of God. I believe that she prayed for me and I believe that she prayed over me. I remember hearing stories about people and their grandmothers praying over them and interceding for them. I believe that to be so true and very powerful because God honors the prayers of the righteous. My grandmother died of cancer in her early 50's. My father said that she used to get happy in church. Well, I am the same way. I am a bit Pentecostal; and I am not ashamed because when the Holy Spirit moves upon me sometimes I cannot contain myself. The presence of God is indescribable!

I am so thankful for my grandmother's life. Even though she did not live very long, I believe God honored her prayers. The Bible says, *"The effectual fervent prayers of the righteous availeth much"* (James 5:16). She was a beautiful woman inside and out.

My neighborhood overall wasn't terrible, but we had some characters who lived among us. I will never forget this one particular, disturbed man who lived a couple doors down from us. Whenever young girls were outside alone, he would chase them. He brought plenty fear to all of the children in the area. He was charged with rape earlier, so we were aware of how dangerous he was. Neighbors would call the police on him, but I guess he always got away due to lack of proof. Just like every other girl, I would always run past his house after leaving a friend's house, and he didn't chase me much. However, my sister Pinky wasn't as fortunate because he always seemed to chase her.

She would be passing his home as he sat on his porch, as if he always knew when she was going to be outside; and from there, it would be a race home for Pinky. My mother, being the protective woman that she was, always was very concerned. The final time he chased Pinky was the day he chased her all the way to the front steps of our house. I was home when I heard the front door swing open and then slam shut! It was Pinky. Sweating and in fear, she caught her breath and told our mother, "Mom, mom, he just chased me again!" Upset, my mother quickly ran up the stairs. I was still in shock and scared for Pinky. My mother came back down the stairs with a gun in her hand. Even being as young as I was and spiritually immature, I still knew to pray. I began to repeat over and over again, "God please calm my mom. Please Lord." In rage, she opened the front door. I just hoped that the man had left. Unfortunately, he was still outside in front of our home. My mother pointed the gun directly at his face and said to him, "I told you to leave my daughter and family alone!" With an evil look in his eyes, he stood there speechless and looked directly back at her. All I could imagine at that time was my mother going to jail. I pleaded with her in tears, "PLEASE DON'T SHOOT HIM, MOM! PLEASE DON'T SHOOT HIM!" He looked at us and turned around and walked away without saying anything. This experience made me that much more frightened to go outside and play. From what we heard he was always in and out of the mental hospital. We always hoped that he would soon find some kind of mental stability but unfortunately, his story ended tragically. Unsure of life, he went on to commit suicide by walking into the Potomac River until the water overtook him to his death.

The Lattisaw Family (from the left): Jerome Jr., Sheila, Jerome Sr. (Dad), Saundra (Mom), Saundra, and Stacy (seated)

Chapter 2

Let the Music Begin

Prior to having children, my mother pursued a music career. She attended high school with the late Marvin Gaye and was one of the lead singers in his group. She was later offered a record deal that ended up falling through; and her singing career never really expanded beyond the local area, but her passion to sing always remained. While doing simple chores, cooking or any other household tasks, my mother would always sing freely. I would always listen and think, *Wow, mom can really sing.* So by the age of 6, I began to mock and imitate the way she sang until it came to the point where we would soon corporately sing harmonies and backgrounds to the other's lead. It was plenty of fun. We would laugh as we sang different tunes. Those were memorable moments I spent with my mother.

Though we had fun and a lot of times I would just be following behind her, she soon recognized that I could actually sing. The more we sang together, I began to open up more and show more vocal ability and she was somewhat surprised at some of the things I could do vocally, coming from such a small, young girl. She began to rave and explain to my father how I could possibly have potential. Sure, he had heard me sing from time to time, but he had never heard me at my best. After being told this, my dad began to listen with a different mindset and agreed that I did have a God given gift. He and my mother talked and decided to shoot for the fame, tours, studio time, live shows, and everything that came with a professional singing career. Because my mother had chased the same dream as a teenager that we would now be after, she knew a couple of the early difficulties of trying to get into this business. There was really only one major difficulty. And it was and is the same difficulty that every other singer in America has who is trying to be a part of the thriving music industry—exposure. The music industry has no definite system of "how to get in." A lot of times, it's simply who you know that can put you in the right positions to have a decent chance of success at this whole thing, and then there's still no guarantee after that. Nevertheless, my father began to record me on a tape recorder and carried a cassette tape of my alone vocals. Once again though, with no connections, we were kind of stuck. However, I began to do different local talent shows and things of that nature, not by choice in the beginning but I would soon adapt.

The first showcase was at Spingarn High School, where my sister Pinky attended. Seeing and recognizing a small opportunity for local exposure, my mother and father signed me up. They told me about it and before they could even finish explaining, I immediately said NO with boldness as if to say, *My mind won't be changed.* I was only about nine years old and my mother knew exactly how to bribe me and change my mind—money. I was offered ten dollars (which was a decent amount of money for a kid back then), and my bold NO turned into a "Well... ok." All I could think about was how many toys I would buy with my ten dollars, so I committed to doing it. Remember, I said yes for the toys and money. This changed nothing about how nervous I felt inside. I was so shy and this would be one of my very first times singing for anybody other than family, not to mention that I would now have to sing in the midst of a couple hundred some odd high school students in a hot muggy auditorium.

Being young and extremely shy created drastic over exaggerations. A crowd of three or four hundred looked like three or four thousand through my eyes. Even the students seemed abnormally large compared to my small nine year old being. The auditorium was dimly lit as the host took the stage and said, "Students of Spingarn, let's put our hands together and welcome the young and talented Stacy Lattisaw." This put even more knots in my stomach as I felt the pressure to now deliver what these people were all anticipating. The music began to play as I took the stage and microphone. I tried my best to put my mother's advice into effect of not looking at anyone in the audience. She told me over and over again, "Stacy, when you get up on that stage, you close your eyes and sing as if it were only you and me in the room." I closed my eyes; and from the beginning of me singing, people began to go haywire as they screamed and clapped. During the song, I would open my eyes slightly to look out below the stage where students had run up to cheer me on.

A lot of God given talents are sometimes doubted and not put into effect simply because of the lack of confidence, and vice versa. I know this to be because once I received that overwhelming response, comfort rose and I sang openly and freely, holding nothing back as if I were back in my kitchen on a regular evening with my mother. I sang two selections that afternoon, so as you can imagine, the second song was no problem at all. My parents were correct in their assumptions, because though this may have just seemed like the average talent show to many, it was local exposure for me. Days later, we began to receive phone calls for me to sing at more talent shows, weddings, and other related events. Because of my parents' lack of knowledge and experience, they felt it was time for them to search for a reputable manager. Then along came Al Dale. Mr. Dale was an established independent music professional in the Washington, DC, area.

One day my mom took me to Fort DuPont Park in Southeast DC where Mr. Dale worked at the time. He was the coordinator for the summer shows there. Each summer there were local and nationally known recording artists who would come there to perform. My mom was determined to meet Mr. Dale so that he could hear me sing. She asked several people, "Where do I find Mr. Dale?" While holding onto my hand, she searched through the crowd and finally made the connection. She introduced herself and said to Mr. Dale, "I want you to hear my daughter sing." Mr. Dale answered, "Sure." He looked at me and asked, "What are you going to sing?" I shrugged my shoulders but I knew what to sing. My mom gave me the confidence that I needed as she always did. So with butterflies in my stomach, I began to sing "Inseparable" by Natalie Cole. Toward the end of the song Mr. Dale looked at my mom and exclaimed, "You have dynamite here." My mom invited Mr. Dale to our home to discuss the possibility of him becoming my manager. After my parents met him, they took a liking to him and decided he was the right man for the job. Mr. Dale was very instrumental in helping me gain exposure through a variety of different events in the area.

One day he called to inform us of an opportunity for me to sing as the opening act for Ramsey Lewis at Fort DuPont Park. Immediately I told my mother no. I said, "I don't want to sing at a park in front of a lot of people." She said, "If I give you twenty dollars, will you do it?" I said, "Yeah I'll do it." I remember as I began to walk up the steps toward the stage I saw thousands and thousands of people. The park was full. The estimated crowd was 30,000 people. Immediately after looking at

the people, I said, "Ma, I can't do this. It's too
many people out there." My mom looked me in
the eyes and replied, "Stacy you can do this." I
remember after the first song I began to feel at
ease. I think I felt more comfortable and confident as well. I sang "This Will Be" and "Mister
Melody" by Natalie Cole. The audience just went
wild. I began to experience what it was really
like to sing in front of large groups of people.

I was just a little girl and I did not really know
what I was doing. I was just up there singing,
without any idea that this would be my career,
a professional singer. That's how it all began.
My aunt Sylvia worked at a cleaners here in the
Washington, DC, area. Her boss was related to
Mr. Jaffey. Mr. Jaffey worked for Atlantic Records
as an attorney. My Aunt Sylvia told Mr. Jaffey's
brother that she wanted him to hear me sing. He
said, "Okay fine, do you have a tape of her? She
answered yes and gave the tape to him to give to
his brother. Mr. Jaffey heard the tape and passed
it along to Mr. Henry Allen, who was the president of Atlantic Cotillion Records. After Mr. Allen
listened to the tape, he asked for me to come to
New York and sing for him in person. My mom,
dad, brother, and I drove there. I sang "You Light
up My Life" by Debbie Boone. As I looked up, Mr.

Allen began to cry. I saw the tears roll down his face and I remember thinking: *Why is he crying?* I didn't understand but obviously he felt something. About two weeks later, I was signed to Atlantic Records. I recorded six albums on Atlantic. I met most of the staff and was somewhat excited. My mom and I often took many trips to New York City. There were always meetings and interviews. New York had almost become our second home.

One of my most exciting memories was meeting Bill Cosby. Henry Allen, my family, and I went to dinner with Mr. Cosby. They took me to this very exquisite restaurant. I didn't understand anything on the menu. All I wanted was pizza and French fries. So needless to say I didn't eat much of anything. I was in search of pizza. Mr. Cosby was very comical; I believe we all laughed more than we talked. Later that day we did a photo shoot together which was on the side of some public buses. It was a photo stating "Don't Smoke." They discussed the possibility of me being one of the daughters on The Cosby Show. So I auditioned for the role of being the oldest sister "Saundra," but obviously I was too shy so I didn't get the part. Acting was never something that I desired or considered so I'm sure it was for the best.

Chapter 3

A Successful Failure

When I was 12 years old, I recorded my very first album entitled "When You're Young and In Love." I really didn't know what I was getting myself into. I just enjoyed singing. It took a lot for me to stand in front of a crowd of people and sing three or four songs, but recording in the studio seemed kind of fun. As I began to get older, I realized my mom wanted to live her dream through me. She always brought out the best in me. Even when I felt nervous she always gave me the confidence that I needed. During this time I was in the studio and I worked with the late Van McCoy. He wrote and produced the entire album. He was very pleasant, and I enjoyed working with him. Van McCoy had a very successful career. He wrote and produced songs for some of the biggest artists in the music industry. One of his greatest hits was "The Hustle."

While recording my first album, I remember feeling a mix of emotions. I was excited and nervous at the same time because I did not know what would come along with all of this. When I stepped into the studio, it looked so big or maybe it was because I was so small. As I recall, when I put the earphones over my head they would not stay on. Because my head was so small, they kept falling off, so I had to hold onto them while I sang. I had already learned the songs so it took very little time to record them.

I completed the entire album in ten days. We recorded two songs a day. Some would say they were bubble gum songs; however, it was difficult to find songs appropriate for a 12-year-old girl. They could not give me love songs or songs that sounded too mature for me. I sang songs like "When You're Young and in Love," "Dreaming," "Downtown," and "Spinning Top." The songs seemed childish, but again they had to be suitable for a little girl. I remember they used to always say, "Wow she is 12, but she sounds older." Even though I sounded older my mom made sure that I looked my age and I appreciate her for that.

A Successful Failure

Growing up, I had a good foundation. My parents were very supportive of me. My dad made a lot of sacrifices for us all. Although he worked a full time job, he was my co-manager. He even traveled with us sometimes but not very much because of his job; somebody had to pay the bills. The more famous I had become the more challenges he faced at work, but he remained strong and confident; he always kept things together. He was and still is the rock of the family. He's a strong man with a good heart, who always put his family first.

Now back to the first album. Most people weren't aware of it because it was a complete flop. Some would think "Let Me Be Your Angel" was my first album, but that was the second one. During this time, I didn't do much travelling. I was still at home with my friends doing normal things that 12-year olds did. We had Atari but we often spent more time playing kickball and volleyball in the front yard, quite often ruining my mother's grass. Even though we ruined her grass most of the time, she preferred that we played in front of our home so that she could keep a close watch on us. I always tried to be well behaved and respectful. I don't recall getting very many spankings because I would see the spankings that my sisters would get and I didn't want any parts of that. Most of the time all it took was a look from my mom and I would know to stop doing whatever it was that I was doing and get it together.

My friends and I would do stupid, yet fun stuff. One of the things we'd do for fun is turn on the fire hydrant in the summer time to cool off from the hot summer days. Of course someone would always call the police, but once they left we'd turn it back on. This was the closest thing that we had to a public swimming pool back then.

I always loved bicycles. Then one day my parents surprised me with the Cadillac of bikes. It was red with white wall tires. Some of my friends would call it a school bus because it was really big. It sat up high in the air. It had a horn and a light. My friends would ask if they could ride and I would share sometimes, but most of the time I would ride my bike until it was nighttime. It was really cool.

Although my first album was not successful and I remained relatively unknown, it really did not affect me very much, because as you can see at that time in my life I just wanted to take pleasure in being a child. After all, you're only a child once!

Chapter 4

Refresh, Renew, Revamp

After the failure of my first album, Mr. Allen decided that he needed to find another producer to write songs that would fit my voice and age. He discovered a young man from San Francisco, California, named Narada Michael Walden. At that time Narada was a professional drummer and an aspiring songwriter and producer; however, he had never produced anyone before. He asked Mr. Allen to give him a shot at producing me because he strongly believed he had the ability to bring out the best in me. Narada came to my home in Southeast Washington, DC, from San Francisco.

My mom bought a piano and placed it in the living room. She was determined to get the best out of me. She wanted me to take piano lessons, but I had no interest at all in the piano. When my piano teacher would come over, I would run somewhere and hide. She also placed me in ballet classes. I had very little interest in ballet as well. My passion was singing because it always came natural to me. During this time Narada would come to our home and bring his songs on a tape recorder and we would sing at the piano for hours. Then one day while playing the piano he came up with a chorus; lo and behold that song became "Let Me Be Your Angel."

Narada Michael Walden and Stacy

At the age of 13 my life began to change because I no longer had a normal childhood. I was unable to do some of the things that typical teenagers could do because "Let Me Be Your Angel" had become a top 10 record. Going places had become difficult, so it was necessary for me to be constantly chaperoned. Being thrust into the limelight at such a young age became a little frightening at times. People used to ride by our home to glance at me. On one occasion my friends and I were outside and a car pulled up with a few people inside. They sat there for a few minutes and began to stare. I was a little frightened so I ran into the house. I was becoming a celebrity and this was quite different for me, because I was always used to going outside and not being bothered.

My home was the after school hangout. After we played and ran around for a while it was time for the talent show. Germain Tyler Graham, one of my best friends, used to model. Another friend, Wendell Kyer, was the comedian. He kept all of us laughing. He was always joking about something; he just laughed about every little thing. I was the singer and my friend Don Bellamy was the actor. Another good friend of mine nicknamed Boogie, better known as Johnny Gill, used to come over to my house almost every day as well. He used to ride his bike over there in a suit. Johnny always wore suits. We never knew that he could sing. We were downstairs one day and he just happened to be over and we asked if he wanted to be in the talent show and he said, "Alright, cool." We asked him if he wanted to dance, sing, or act. He said he wanted to sing a song. I cannot remember what song it was, but I ran upstairs and told my mother that Boogie could sing. I said, "You have got to hear him sing because his voice is just amazing!" He did not have the voice of a teenager; he had the mature voice of a man.

She came downstairs to hear him sing. Her response was "Oh my goodness, we have got to let Henry hear him sing." My mom called Mr. Allen and told him about this young boy with a grown man's voice. We told Johnny to make a tape and send it to him. After hearing Johnny sing, Mr. Allen signed him on to Atlantic Records. Johnny recorded his first solo album; and we later did a duet album that was entitled "Perfect Combination." Although "Perfect Combination" did not generate a high volume of record sales, in my opinion it was one of the most beautiful collection of songs. It was top 10 on the billboard charts and it jumpstarted Johnny Gill's career.

It is amazing how people never forget your music. I really believe good music has a way of lasting. You can hear a song one day and ten years later that same song still sounds great. I had lots of favorite songs that, in my opinion, were wasted. Songs like "My Love, I've Loved You Somewhere Before," I Could Love You So Divine," He's Got a Hold on Me," "Long Shot" and "He's Just Not You." Unfortunately, I never had much say about which songs were chosen as singles. I have often thought if I had more input perhaps things would have been different. But God had a plan.

I have had some regrets and complaints in my life, but there are no coincidences or accidents in God! He sees all things; we don't. We see our yesterdays, but He sees our tomorrows. Times were a little tough when I was growing up, but we always had the best Christmases. I don't ever recall not getting something that I asked for on my Christmas list. My parents would tell us that they were going to see Santa to tell him what we wanted for Christmas. Quite naturally when they returned we would always pretend that we were asleep. I would always hear the sound of plastic bags and I couldn't help but to get out of bed to try and sneak a peep but I would always get caught. Okay, I'll be the first to admit that I've always been nosey. I like to know what's going on and I don't like surprises!

I'm reminded of two funny but scary stories when I got caught for being nosey. My sister Pinky's boyfriend came to see her and they were downstairs in the basement. I wanted to see what they were doing so I opened the door to the basement and fell down the stairs. I seem to have missed every step as my head hit the floor I began to scream to the top of my lungs as my mom rushed me to the hospital. Fortunately, I didn't break any bones. I just bumped my head. On another occasion I was trying to listen in on a conversation that my mother was having with my brother. I just knew he was in big trouble. As I put my head to the door, they opened the door and I fell onto the floor; then I had become the one in trouble for being nosey again.

Chapter 5

School Days

When I was in the eighth grade, things were kind of normal at school, but then again they weren't, because there were a few teachers who started to give me a hard time. I was always very shy and somewhat timid. Because I was quiet most of the time, people sometimes took it the wrong way. I didn't have many friends at school and I often felt prejudged. They said things like "She thinks she's cute or she's stuck up." They would label me as being this conceited person, but I wasn't. I was just reserved.

Middle School

I remember a particular teacher who definitely gave me a hard time. She was my history teacher. I think jealousy was the case with her, because she picked on me for no reason. One day we took a test and she told me that she couldn't find mine. I remembered that I had definitely turned it in. So I went home and said to my mother, "Ma, I don't know why this lady is giving me such a hard time. I don't think she likes me; she just doesn't like me." So my mother said, "I'm going to the school to find out what is going on." My mother scheduled a meeting with my teacher to try and resolve any problems. My mother told her that she knew I was a quiet girl and she wanted to know what was going on. Unfortunately this teacher had a bad attitude and she and my mother had words, but thankfully my father was there. If he had not been, there is no telling what could have happened, because mama Lattisaw doesn't play.

During this period some girls had started to pick on me. They used to call me white girl, yellow girl, and red girl. I never responded. I would just put my head down and keep walking down the hall. I remember a girl used to sit behind me and pull my hair almost every single day. I told the teacher, Mr. Harrison, that she kept teasing me and pulling my hair. He told her to stop pulling my hair, but she would not stop. She just kept on. Quite frankly, I was afraid of her because she was very tall and big. I was this short, skinny girl just minding my business. Then one day I got to the point where I was fed up. I came home and I told my mom. She made a special visit to the school. She tried talking to the teacher hoping he could resolve it, but the girl kept picking on me. So my mom had a little talk with the girl and it worked. She left me alone and never bothered me again. In fact she never even looked at me again. Unfortunately being light skinned was not easy for me. Some people tend to not like you because of the color of your skin. Hummm....some things don't change. For many years after I dealt with some of the same issues. I thank God for my big sister Pinky because on many occasions she was my protector. She wasn't going to let anyone mess with her little sister. She always had my back.

As I became more popular, my parents decided that home school would be best for me. They asked me how I felt about it. I said, "Home school? What does that mean?" My mother responded, "You just stay at home and a teacher will come to our home and teach you. I think that is what we are going to do, because the more popular you become it may become difficult to stay in school and learn." They wanted me to get a good education and be safe, so it was the best decision for me. However, being home schooled and away from my friends made me feel sad and alone. My tutor came to my home every day and I completed my high school years at home. That was a depressing time for me, because I never got a chance to go to my high school prom, dances, or football and basketball games.

Not long ago, I took my son to a high school football game. I said, "Wow, I can't believe I actually missed times like this." I was in the car watching them play football at his school and I thought, *Those times for me were supposed to be fun, but they were not.* That was a sacrifice I had to make. It came with the territory of being a so-called child star. I can definitely relate to Michael Jackson and some of the things that he may have gone through, because he was very young when he started singing. Being a child star means you cannot do some of the things that normal kids do. Something as little as going to the ice cream truck by myself wasn't possible. My parents were very cautious. I did not understand why they were so protective but I certainly appreciate it now. My dad's friend, Bob Pitts, who was my road manager and body guard, would always take me and my friends to the skating rink and the go cart track. He is six feet five inches tall, so nobody ever bothered me when Bob was around.

When I was 15 and a half years old, it was almost time for me to get my driver's license. Because my mom was so strict, she was not in favor of it, but my dad was in my corner. He said, "Let's just trust her." I was able to buy my first car. I paid cash for a Chrysler Lebaron convertible. I remember my friends and I would put the top back in the winter. We would ride around the neighborhood freezing cold, but it was the best!

At 16, Johnny and I began to date; we dated for about 4 years. We spent a lot of time together, going to the movies and out to eat. I enjoyed his company. Johnny and I would laugh about everything. And we would talk on the phone until we both fell asleep. I met his sweet mom, Mrs. Gill, and the rest of his family. We were all pretty close. I attended church with them quite often. Many times Johnny would sing at church. I recall one Sunday he sang a song without a microphone and his voice just lit up the church. Tears were streaming down his face as he sang. It just moved me to tears because I felt something special about him. I know now that it was the anointing. Johnny is gifted and anointed, and I still believe that he has a calling on his life!

We have a mutual friend named Keith Martin. Keith and I used to make hot dogs on the grill in the winter. We burnt them every time. I still like my hotdogs burnt. Johnny and Keith would crack jokes on each other. We'd be on the floor laughing so hard that our stomachs would hurt.

In 1983 my family purchased a beautiful home in Forest Heights, MD. It seemed like a mansion compared to where we used to live. Our home consisted of thirteen rooms. The back yard was beautiful, filled with lots of trees and a big swimming pool. Although I never learned how to swim, I enjoyed getting in the pool for fun and relaxation. However there was one thing I did not like about that area. There were lots of snakes. I often ate dinner out back near the pool until I saw a snake one day. I dropped my plate and ran inside. Needless to say, I am a little afraid of snakes. I choose to keep my distance. During this time we had an Afghan named Uno and for some strange reason he barked a lot at night. And because my bedroom was in the rear of our home, his bark obviously would awaken me. As I think about it now, he was probably barking at a snake that we later found hiding in one of the storage containers outside of my window.

We often had pool parties. Pinky had a party one night and Tommy Davidson and Martin Lawrence were there. We had a blast! However, some of her friends had too much to drink and they began throwing each other in the pool. Things began to get a little bit out of control so my dad had to ask a few people to leave. We lived in a somewhat quiet neighborhood, so quite naturally someone called the police because of the loud music. We tried to keep the music down but someone kept turning it back up. When the police arrived they didn't give us a hard time. In fact one of them stayed for while and joined in on the fun. They just requested that we turn the music down.

CHAPTER 6

Show Time

Show time is when I began to sing and do live performances at big venues such as convention centers, arenas, and similar places. I shared the stage with people such as Natalie Cole, Aretha Franklin, and a host of others. I recall a time when Natalie Cole, Sister Sledge, my mom, and I went to dinner at a seafood restaurant in Atlanta, Georgia. I think we ordered almost everything on the menu. The food was great but the mini concert was even better. Natalie began to tap on the table with the crab knocker making a beat. Then she began to sing as Sister Sledge and I joined in. The people in the restaurant were excited. Some of them joined in and sang with us. We had a ball! That was the best impromptu concert I've ever been in.

In 1980, I was the opening act for Teddy Pendergrass on several shows. I also did shows with Stephanie Mills and variety of well-known artist back in the mid 1980's. Those were very stressful times for me at 15 and 16 years old. I had to perform three or four nights a week. Whew! That was tough because having to be in two to three different cities in a week required a lot of flying on airplanes. My mother traveled everywhere with me. She never let me travel alone.

Then came the panic attacks. The stress was becoming too much for us. We both suffered with panic attacks. One day the record company gave me an album release party and my mother did not feel well. She asked one of the representatives from the record label to take her to the doctor. When she returned she told us the doctor explained that it was a panic attack. She was just under so much stress. In 1983 we went to Japan. I performed at The Yahama Musical Festival. It was a talent showcase where artist from all around the world came to perform. I sang "Longshot," one of my favorite songs, and won first prize. I was presented with a Rado watch and ten thousand dollars. That was an awesome event. In 1984 we went to Africa. I was the opening act for Connie Francis. That was definitely the longest flight I had ever been on. We spent over twenty hours on the airplane. It was a great experience, but it just took us forever to get there.

Pinky had just had her first child, Toyia (the spoiled one). She was the first grandchild in the family so I wanted to stay home and be with her. I wanted to help my sister raise her, so I cried a lot when it was time for us to hit the road. We've always been a close family so being away from home, family, and friends made me very unhappy at times. Some people do not get the opportunity to travel like I had at a young age, but it came with a price.

Jerry used to sing the backgrounds on "Love on A Two Way Street." At the time he was ten years old and was not shy at all. He later formed an R&B group called Prophet Jones and signed a record deal with Motown Records. He has an incredible voice with a wide range. Jerry still loves to sing. Not long ago we were singing old songs together and it brought back lots of memories about our childhood. He's a grown man now but he'll always be my baby brother.

When I turned sixteen I got a huge surprise. I was at home one day and Michael Jackson called to wish me a happy birthday. I did not believe that it was him. He whispered, "Hello, may I speak to Stacy?" and I replied, "Uumm, who is this?" He announced his name and at first I did not believe him, but it was him. I chuckled, "Wow this really is Michael. This really is him." I was thrilled! Michael Jackson calling me!!!? I was blown away! My parents gave me a sweet sixteen birthday party and it was so much fun, because my dad rented a tour bus that we took over to the NCO Club at one of the local military bases. My father's friend, Mr. Ellis, helped to make that possible. It was amazing! We just danced and sang. It was great!

Not long after that, my dad received a phone call from Michael Jackson's manager requesting that I be the opening act for the Victory Tour. My first response was "No," because the tour would last for 13 weeks. I was definitely not in favor of it. I said no immediately, but of course my management and my parents talked me into it. They told me that this would take my career to another level. It was indeed an honor for me because not many people had been given the opportunity to tour with, in my opinion, the greatest entertainer of all time, Michael Jackson. It was a tremendous opportunity. I was able to go backstage and talk with Michael after the shows. My brother Jerry and I watched every show. That was an awesome experience.

I would watch the people's reaction when Michael performed. Some of the fans would cry, yell, and dance while some would even faint from the excitement. There were ambulances parked on each side of the building. Wow! That's the type of effect he had on some people. He was incredibly gifted. The way he danced and moved was phenomenal. He was the best! We were able to meet all of the Jackson family—their parents, Jermaine, Marlon, Randy, Jackie, Tito, Latoya, and Janet. I will never forget those times and I cherish those moments with Michael Jackson and being able to talk with him. He was shy and so was I, so we did not talk very much, but we did communicate sometimes after the shows. I still think at times *Wow, they asked me to be the opening act!* As I look back on it now, God allowed that door to be open for me and it definitely took my career to another level. At that time, I was able to purchase a lot of nice things but I still had no real peace within.

On two different occasions I was invited to the White House. My first visit was in 1980 when President Jimmie Carter was in office. I had the opportunity to meet him and his daughter Amy

Carter. President Carter was very kind. Amy was very nice and soft spoken. She and I talked for a few minutes then she invited me to her bedroom. It was absolutely beautiful. The colors were bright and pretty. It was a bedroom fit for a princess. She asked me what type of music I sang and I told her R&B. I handed her my single and she played it on her jukebox. I remember thinking *I'd like to have one of those.* We continued to laugh and talk for a while until it was time for us to go. Amy and I never kept in touch but it was a pleasure meeting her. My second visit was in 1986 when President Ronald Reagan was in office. I had the pleasure of meeting the first Lady, Mrs. Nancy Reagan. She presented me with a certificate for being a positive role model for teenagers.

As I'm sitting here writing this book, it's brought back many memories. I must say that I am very humbled by the opportunities that God has given me. I hold those special times dear to my heart. Because I was so young at that time, I did not realize what a privilege it was for me to meet President Carter, his daughter Amy Carter, and Mrs. Reagan, and to tour with the Jacksons.

Michael Jackson and Stacy Lattisaw

Chapter 7

Independence

When I was almost 18, I was pretty much an adult, so my mother had no choice but to let me go and date. I never did any type of drugs. I thank God that He kept me from those types of vices. Sometimes people in the entertainment industry tend to gravitate to drugs and alcohol because of the stress. When I was under 18, my money went into a trust fund and my legal guardians at the time were my parents. They handled all my finances, paid all my bills, and took care of everything for me. When I turned 18, I had access to all my money and my parents were no longer my legal guardians per se. Finally, I was able to do pretty much whatever I wanted to do with my money.

I bought my first pet, an Amazon Parrot. I named him Alfie. He was very big and pretty. The pet store owner told me he could learn to talk. I began to spend time with him. I would sing to him and say little things over and over again. It took some time but he began to repeat everything I said. He would say things like "Have you been a good birdie" and "Oh baby." I would put him on my shoulder while walking around the house and sing to him. Then he began to sing with this amazing vibrato. I used to hear him sing and think, *Wow, this bird can sing. He laughs just like me and sounds just like me when he talks.* Alfie was always very friendly, but I noticed he was starting to change. He was becoming very mean and aggressive and I didn't know what to do.

During this time I began to lose focus on my bird because my money had started to disappear. I knew I had made a lot of money, but I wondered what happened to it. I did not understand what was going on. My dad hired an accountant for me and he handled my taxes. He was supposed to take care of everything, but obviously he did not. Money had been paid out and mishandled on my behalf for taxes, booking agents, accountants and managers. Because of the amount of money I was earning, I found myself in a 50 percent tax bracket. My management company failed to set up any good tax shelters for me. That would have helped me tremendously, but unfortunately that was not the case. To top it all off, I later found out that the same management company had somehow stolen money from one of my recording budgets. Although they stole the money, because I was the artist I had to pay it back to the record company.

In 1989 I recorded a duet with Johnny Gill titled "Where Do We Go from Here," which was my last single and a number one hit song. At this point I decided to walk away from R&B. I got really tired of the record company not supporting me. I came to realize that they were not really giving me the attention or the respect that I believed I deserved. I began to lose my desire to sing R&B music. I went to my dad one day and I mumbled, "Dad I don't know what's going on with me, but I don't think that I am going to sing R&B much longer." What really put the icing on the cake for me was the duet being number one on the billboard charts. Johnny and I were told that the album only sold 30 thousand copies. I found that very hard to accept and believe.

We were just blown away because we knew the song was number one for 4 weeks; and we refused to believe that it could have sold only 30 thousand copies. I remember Johnny was really upset about it. He decided that he was going to get an attorney to find out exactly what happened. I was disgusted. I felt as if they were not in my favor. I became more and more frustrated and unhappy in the music industry, so I just decided to walk away. Most people would ask, "Why would you walk away from the music business with a number one single?"

Chapter 8

Spiritual Awakening

I had become very unhappy with where I was in my life; and I felt as though I was just at a stand-still. Of course, the void was still there and I was trying to fill it with stuff—clothes, shoes, purses, rings and diamonds, and things—but I always felt a void on the inside. I knew of God, but I did not have a relationship with Him. We were raised as Catholic. For a long time, my mom and I used to go to a Catholic Church because we felt that it was the right thing to do, but we weren't growing spiritually.

One day I decided to go to a Baptist Church. I felt that I needed to dig a little deeper and find out who God is for myself. I dropped to the floor and

I pleaded, "God I need to know You for myself. I need to know who You are. I heard about You; and I need to know that You are real." I felt a presence that I had never felt before in my life. It was as if God had spoken these words to me, "That's it. I have been waiting on you for a long time and now that you are here, I am going to show you who I am. I am going to show you My will for you and My plans for you." Things began to change for me. I went to my dad and announced, "Dad I don't know what's going to happen to me. I don't know how I am going to pay my bills, but I know, that I know, that I heard from God; and I will no longer be singing R&B music." My dad asked, "Are you sure you know what you are talking about? And I answered, "Dad, I believe; and I know that God is real and He has other plans for my life."

A lot of people did not understand why I walked away from the music business, but I had to follow God's instructions. I had to seek His face and not His hands. I sought the face of God every day. To be successful in life requires being in the center of God's will. This is a place of security and blessing! If we are desirous about being in the will of God, we will be! The key is desire! So I began to pray in the dark on my knees, on my face before God. I would cry out to Him, and I would ask Him to just show me His will for my life and to give me more of His presence and His peace. When I experienced the presence of God it changed my whole outlook on life. It was like I had tapped into something. I had an experience. I had an encounter with God. At that moment, the Lord began to change my desires. He began to change my heart. I stopped doing the things I used to do and I stopped going to the places I used to go. I just wanted to be where God was. I wanted to spend time with Him, get to know Him, read His Word and learn of Him. That is when Stacy began to change. Stacy was no longer the same person. God's presence began to take over; and He began to show me things about myself.

God revealed to me that there was unforgiveness in my heart toward someone who had hurt me. I thought I had let it go but it was still there. He dealt with me about it and I released it to Him. Sometimes we think that we have it altogether, but when we go to God He begins to show us who we really are. He begins to let us see ourselves in the mirror. He shows us what's on the inside. God is not concerned about what we look like; He's more concerned about the inward man. He dealt with me about pride. When you are a celebrity people tend to put you up on a pedestal. They would say, "You are Stacy Lattisaw. What are you doing living in Maryland? Aren't you supposed to be in California or New York?" But I loved being at home with my family. Family has always been important to me.

I just turned it all over to God and I sought Him and sought Him. The more time I spent with Him the more I began to change. Glory to God! God began to strip me and put me in the fire. The Bible says, *"He who suffers in the flesh has ceased from sin"* (1 Peter 4:1). I suffered for some time. I no longer had money coming in from the record company and I was no longer performing. I still had bills to pay and I still had responsibilities. I declared, "God I have to trust You; I have to believe beyond where I am. And I know that if You took the desire to sing R&B away from me, then You are going to take care of me. You are going to provide for me in another way." Hallelujah! God began to do just that. I'm so glad that our God never leaves us where He finds us. He almost doubled my husband's income in a way where he was able to take care of me and provide for our family. Well, it's been 17 years and He has taken care of me. He has proven to be my Jehovah Jireh! He told me that He would send me out in His time; and I would go back and minister to some of the same people that I sang R&B to and they would not see Stacy Lattisaw, but they would see Him. Glory to God!

I bless God for being who He is, because for every tear I cried and every dark place that I was in for so long—that dark place that I could not seem to find my way out of—God was there all the time. His hand was upon me and He was closer to me than I even realized, because I felt so alone. I felt like, *God where are you? I know that you are real, but I don't feel Your presence; and I need to know who You are. I need to know You for myself."* As time went on, God revealed more and more of Himself to me. I treasure those times because they have made me who I am today. It made me trust Him and take Him at His Word and to know Him as my provider; to know Him as my healer; to know Him as my deliverer; to know Him as my way maker; and to know Him in a whole different way because He is the God who is more than enough. He said that His grace is sufficient for me.

During that time, I even lost my hair. I had a terrible fungus infection in my scalp. I went to the doctor and he said these words to me, "You might want to have an AIDS test done because I have never seen an infection this bad before." The Lord used my mom's friend Matia, who is a prophet, to speak into my life. She prophesied these words to me, "The Lord instructed "As you begin to praise and worship Me I will heal your scalp." I thank God for placing Matia in my life. She is my prayer partner, a true woman of God.

I did not understand what was going on at the time. I did not have a clue as to what praise and worship was all about. I did not know what to do. All I knew to do was to do what any other person would do and that was to look at the situation. I kept on looking at myself. I would take a hand mirror and go to another mirror and look at my scalp. The more I looked at it the worse it got. I did not understand because the medicine was not working. I even thought about what the doctor told me about having an AIDS test done. I feared, *Oh my Lord! Is this what it could be?* All kinds of things were going through my mind at the time, but it was not until one day I remembered hearing this voice say to me, "But you are not doing what I told you to do. I told you to begin to praise and worship Me and that I will heal your scalp."

At that moment, I started to do what He said to do. I followed His instructions and I put the mirror down. I began to praise and worship God. I began to listen to worship music and I just

worshipped God and worshipped Him and worshipped Him. It took some time, but God healed
my scalp and He restored my hair. I am a witness
to the healing power of God. When I went back to
the doctor, he exclaimed, "Wow, what happened
to your scalp? It looks much better." I remember
I looked in his eyes and I said, "The Lord Jesus
healed my scalp. He took the fungus away." I give
God all the glory for that. He was not only teaching me the power of praise and worship, but He
was teaching me obedience to follow Him instead
of my mind, instead of what my thoughts sug-
gested to do. I was growing and I am still growing
in the Lord, but I followed God's instructions and
He healed my scalp.

Chapter Nine

Mrs. Mom

During this time I began to date my sound engineer, Kevin Jackson. My dad introduced us. I think it was a setup. I could tell my dad really liked him, but at the time I was dating someone else. I used to flirt with him and call him cutie pie. He asked me out a few times and I declined because I thought he was engaged to someone. We became friends and eventually I gave in and we went on our first date to Pizza Hut. He owned Jackson Sound and Lights Company and Night Flight Recording Studio. He was a recording engineer, songwriter, and record producer. He and his partner, Rick White, wrote and produced songs together for Tanya Blount, 2DExtreme, Prophet

Jones, Gladys Knight and Dave Hollister. He also mixed songs for such artists as Deitrick Haddon, Gerald Levert, Genuine, Fred Hammond, Marvin Sapp, Donald Lawrence, and a host of others.

As time went on Kevin's schedule became overwhelming, so he decided to let the light company go and put more focus on writing and producing records. Kevin is the youngest of his four brothers and one sister. One of his older brothers (Aaron) passed away a few years ago. Even though Kevin is the youngest of his siblings, he always had a great deal of confidence and leadership. The more time I spent with him the more I realized he was becoming more than a friend. I began to share with him some of my hurts and disappointments from prior relationships. I dated a few young men years ago, but there was something about Kevin that was unlike any of them. He was very sincere and he loved me because of who I was inside, not THE STACY LATTISAW.

After about six months into our dating we became engaged, and in the next six months we were married. We had a very small wedding at our church on a Monday night with just family and close friends. I knew in my heart that my dad was happy for me, but I also knew that it was hard for him to let me go. He held my hand as he walked me down the aisle. When it was time for him to let go of my hand, my mom smiled and pulled his hand away. I guess he felt like he was losing his baby girl, but we're still close. In fact after Kevin and I got married, my parents decided that they would make dinner on Sundays. To this day, we go to my parents' house every Sunday for dinner. We laugh, talk, and enjoy each other's company. That's what family is about—spending time with the ones you love.

If you have aught with a parent or family member in your life, I encourage you to try and make peace. Reach out to them because life is too short. Even if you've been hurt by someone, pray and ask God to help you release it. You can get past the hurt and be free. God wants us to live a life free from bondage, but if we don't acknowledge the unforgiveness then we can become defeated. The Bible says in John 10:10, *"The thief cometh not, but for to steal, and to kill, and to destroy."* You will never experience God's best while holding unforgiveness in your heart. If we learn to pray and give our hurts, disappointments, and unforgiveness to God, He will not only release the pain, but He will also give us compassion for others who have also been hurt.

71

There are three very important things we must do in order to be free from unforgiveness. First, we must acknowledge the unforgiveness. Next, it's important to ask God to help us to forgive that person or persons who have hurt us. In most cases this is a process, but as we continue to pray God will enable us to forgive. Finally, we must release it to God. The grace of God is incredible. It enables us to do what we cannot do on our own. John 8:36 says, *"He whom the Son sets free is free indeed."* Don't let unforgiveness steal your joy because if you have no joy, you have no strength. If you have no strength then you will not be effective for God's use. It all begins with love. So if there is unforgiveness in your heart, release it to God today and begin to walk in liberty. You will no longer be a victim, but the victor!

After Kevin and I had been married for about a year I became pregnant with our only son, Kevin Jr., who is now 17 years old. Having a child definitely changed my life. It was no longer the same. I remember when I used to be able to get up and go when I wanted to, take baths when I wanted to, eat when I wanted to and sleep when I wanted to; but all of that began to change. I must admit when I don't get enough sleep I am a little cranky. When I became a mother, my focus was on my children: raising them, nurturing them, teaching them, and instilling the things of God in them. I believe that God intended for us as parents to raise our children in the fear and the admonition of Him. *"A child left to himself will bring his mother to shame"* (Proverbs 29:15). It is amazing how that Scripture specifically says mother. Hmmm!! I believe that being a mother is a great responsibility; and most of the time, children tend to call their mothers first whenever there is a problem. There is a special bond that a mother has with her children.

Sometimes we as parents tend to forget that parenting does not start at school. It does not start outside the home. It starts in the home. It is our responsibility as parents to teach our children the things of God at a young age. When they begin to talk, we should begin to teach them who God is, the importance of prayer, and the importance of having God in their life. These are things that we should instill in our children. I believe that we can do that much more effectively than someone else can. So that is my role as a parent. About two and a half years after Kevin, Jr. was born, our daughter Kayla was born. Kayla is now 13. I have two teenagers, which is quite different. Whew! Teenagers are more mature nowadays and we as parents are in a place now where we have to begin to trust them as they become older. We have to know that we have instilled the right things in them so as they begin to get older, they can make good choices. Even though they may not make the right choices all of the time, it is a part of growing and learning. But it's so very important for them to learn from those mistakes and to not repeat them.

When I was pregnant with Kayla, I had problems off and on. During the first trimester the doctor explained how he could not find her heartbeat and had me to come back for another sonogram. I was so upset. I called Kevin and he came home right away. I was crying and I was afraid because I did not know what to do; but I prayed with my prayer partner Matia. I had to trust God. I recall another time during my pregnancy I used to have pains off and on in my stomach. I went to the doctor and he thought it was nothing. He recommended that I drink a little ginger ale and said that it would probably go away. Just before Kayla was born I had another sonogram and found out that I had gallstones. I carried her full term but I had to have a Cesarean section. Then six weeks later my gallbladder was removed. That was so difficult and painful to me, physically and emotionally, because she was a newborn baby of six weeks and I could not hold her the way I wanted to. God kept me in the midst of it all. As I look back on it now, I understand that it is all about trust. It is all about taking God at His Word. I had to walk by faith, not by sight. There are times in our lives when He knows that we need help. We can't run this race alone. We all need people to encourage us, pray with us, and pray for us. I am so thankful for Matia. Her walk with God has impacted many lives. God has used her tremendously in my life.

As Christians, we ought to live the life that we talk about because our walk with God is more effective than our talk about God. I remember reading an article titled *"Are we followers of God or are we fans of God?"* That really ministered to me because there really is a difference between the two. If we become followers of God then we can make a difference. Followers of God are also committed to Him and serve Him with their life. It's all about the way we live.

I always tell this story about love and how God sees us and loves us. A few years ago I was out in Washington, DC, and a young man recognized me and asked me for my autograph. He may have been homeless or maybe he had not bathed for a couple of days, because he had a foul odor and he looked unclean. He asked me for a hug and I said, "Yes, sure you can hug me." He said, "Thank you. It was really nice meeting you. It was a pleasure." That to me is an example of love, because if we cannot love the unlovable and touch the untouchable, then how are we representing God? God is love and we may say, "Well I'm not going to touch that person, because he's homeless;" or "I'm not going to let him come near me." Just a smile or an encouraging word could bless someone. That is who our God is. He is love. If we cannot be an example of love, then who are we?

I count it an honor to know God and to have a relationship with Him as opposed to religion. God wants a relationship with His people. It is an honor to go to God in prayer and seek His face. He just wants us to spend time with Him; He wants us to commune with Him. We do not even have to say anything when we come into His presence because He already knows our needs. What He wants us to do is give Him time—just sit at His feet. Psalm 16:11 says, *"In the presence of the Lord, there is fullness of joy."* As we come into His presence, He meets us there. He loves on us and we love on Him. We all must have a secret place— a place where we meet with God and He meets with us. For me, my secret place is at home in my closet. My kids know that when I am in that closet and the door is closed that is my time with God. That is when I am communing with Him and He is communing with me.

Find your secret place wherever it may be— your bathroom, your closet, your car, or your basement, wherever it maybe. God is always available. When we spend time in the presence of God, we begin to take on the character of God. Not only that, but God changes us when we are in His presence. He removes the burdens and the cares of the world because as we begin to worship Him, it totally takes our focus off ourselves and the cares of life and puts our focus on Him.

Praise and worship are so important to me. That is how we begin our day. When I take my daughter to school in the morning, we worship. I believe that worship sets the atmosphere and that is the best way to start your day. It just sets the tone for the day and it puts your focus immediately on Him and not on your plans for the day. Begin your day with worship because that is totally focusing on Him, His omniscience, His sovereignty, His holiness, His faithfulness, His grace, and His mercy. Worship is just so much needed. I cannot imagine living my life without the Lord.

The Bible says that God loves us, but sin separates us from Him.

We, as Christians, must get to a place where we must love God more, deny ourselves, and ask God to give us the grace to live holy. Holiness and worship are a lifestyle. It's the way we live our lives and represent Him. We can worship God in the way that we live. Treating others right represents God. Living a life of integrity represents God. Loving one another represents God. It is an act of worship when we do kind things to people and give a kind word of encouragement. I am learning more and more about the importance of worship. Praise is our weapon and worship is our connection. When you begin to worship Him, He shows you great and mighty things. In His presence is an unspeakable joy. Hallelujah!!

Quite often God uses my kids to minister to me. When my son started high school, I wanted to have him transferred to another school. I called the county to see if it was possible because the school that he was supposed to attend, from what I heard, was one of the worst schools in the county. I remember saying, "God, I don't want him at that school." I cried and I prayed. I said, "Lord, please fix it so he can go to another school if it so be Your will." We were coming home from dinner one evening and a song titled "Let Go and Let God" came on the radio. That song really ministered to me. It was as if God was saying, "I have this! I know that you are concerned about it, but I have this. I know all about it. I know exactly what is going on in this school."

I heard that there was a lot of fighting and the kids were running over the principal and the teachers. I just heard so many negative things about the school. I remember the Lord used Kev to speak to me. He knew that I really did not want him at that school. He said, "Mom, I prayed about it and you know what, I'm okay with going to that school. Just think about it this way, if God wants me to go to that school, he might use me the same way that He used Moses. He could use me to bring positive change to that school." God used him supernaturally; it was like a burden lifted from me. I was amazed how God used him to speak to me and encourage me letting me know that God had it. Wow! It is both amazing and a blessing how God can use our children to minister to us.

There were two different occasions when God used Kayla. There was a promoter I worked with a few years ago who put together a gospel concert. Kayla said, "Mom, it's something about him. I don't think that you should trust him. I don't think that you should do the concert." She was only 10 at that time. Obviously she felt something about him. I remember telling her, "Kayla, its okay. He's a nice guy; he seems to be alright so I am going to do the show." Unfortunately things did not go as well as I had hoped. I was never paid the remaining balance of what was owed to me. That was a weird situation; maybe I should have listened to my daughter. God worked it out and it is okay now. She has the gift of discernment.

There was another situation when my daughter was in elementary school. She was walking down the hall one day and found a twenty dollar bill. She did not know what to do with it, but she knew it did not belong to her. She figured that someone had lost their lunch money, so she put it in her pocket and went to her teacher and told her that she had found the money in the hallway and wanted to see who it belonged to. She gave it to her teacher, who said that she would give it to the principal and see who may have lost it. Kayla did the right thing and I am thankful that she did. After she went to the teacher, she came back to me and said, "Mom I wonder if the teacher is going to keep the money; or if she is going to give it to the principal like she said that she was going to do." I told her, "Don't you worry about that part because you did what was right in the sight of God; so God is going to take care of it. You did the right thing. That was integrity that you showed, because you could have kept the money. You didn't have to say anything about it but you chose to do the right thing." A few days later God blessed her. He gave her the exact amount of money back that she had turned in to her teacher. She came home from school one day to our studio and there was someone there who was doing a recording session. After he paid for his session, he handed her a twenty dollar bill.

Once he left, I asked Kayla where she thought the money came from. She answered, "God." I asked her, "Why do you think God gave you twenty dollars?" She did not say anything; and I told her, "It's because you did what was right. God says that we reap what we sow. He showed you that you did the right thing. He honored your faithfulness. He honored your desire to do right." The Bible says God sees and rewards us for the things that we do. Hallelujah! Glory to God! He rewards us openly for the things that we do in private. Hallelujah! So He rewarded her. He showed her another stepping stone of His faithfulness. That is the kind of God we serve. He is sovereign. He never sleeps and He never slumbers. Hallelujah!

I'm so thankful that both of my kids have a relationship with God.

One day when Kayla was at school the lights went out. Some of the kids started screaming; and some of them jumped up and ran around. I asked her what she did. She replied, "I called Jesus." The fact that she knew to call Him first really blessed me. I am reminded of another occasion when my son was sick. I was in the kitchen making breakfast and he yelled, "Mom, come here." I went upstairs and he was on the floor praying. I asked him what was wrong. He said that he was praying because he didn't feel good. It blessed my soul to see him look to God, and to go to God directly for himself and pray. Hallelujah! He knew to pray.

Those are little blessings that I wanted to share to show God's love and faithfulness. I remember Matia saying, "Stacy, it's such a blessing that your kids know God at such a young age." That is true because knowing God when you are young will help you to make good choices in life. The bad choices that you make today may bring on bad results or consequences in your future. Instilling the word of God in your children when they are young is important because that has great rewards for you as a parent. It is rewarding for them as well because they will know God for themselves. They're not perfect kids but they do know God. To me leaving a legacy is when they see you pray and walk upright before God.

I remember hearing a preacher say a long time ago that most likely your kids are going to do what they see you do and they are going to say what they hear you say. I find that to be so, so true. Sometimes I say things like "Lord, help my life." Sometimes my kids laugh and joke about it, but they are starting to say that, too. Another thing I often say is, "Good God from Zion." Sometimes Kev will jokingly mimic me, but one day he is going to get the Holy Ghost and he will experience what I am talking about for himself.

Now back to my husband Kevin and our marriage. He is a wonderful husband and dad. We do not have a perfect marriage. I do not believe there will ever be a perfect marriage because we are not perfect people. No one is perfect. Everyone has flaws. We all have our weaknesses. We all do things or say things sometimes that we should not do or say. Our pastor once said one of the secrets to a successful marriage is two forgiving people. I have found that to be so true. I believe it's when we learn to forgive and forget. I have heard people say that they can forgive, but they

cannot forget. Those two go hand-in-hand, because if you cannot forgive, you cannot forget;
and if you cannot forget, you cannot forgive. As
we learn to forgive we walk in love. The day I told
Kevin that I did not think I would be singing R&B
music any longer he assured me that he would
support my decision. God saw his heart and He
saw mine; that is why He placed us together. We
are one. Kevin was always raised to be the bread
winner. His father, the late James Jackson, left a
lasting impact on his life; and his mother Gloria
Jackson is very loving and generous. She contin-
ues to be the backbone of the family.

Kevin and I have been married for eighteen
years. He has helped to make a lot of my dreams
come true. He's not only my husband, but he's
my best friend. He's a God-fearing man—a man
with integrity and a great big heart! I am thankful that he saw fit to trust God to take care of us.
I remember when we began dating, Kevin did not
attend church regularly so that was something
that I had to pray about. One Sunday I asked him
to come to church with me and he agreed to visit. After the sermon was over, my pastor asked
if there was anyone who requested prayer. Kevin
stood up and began to walk down the aisle. As I
sat there I heard a voice speak to me, "*He's going*

to be your husband." I was thinking where did that come from? Because we had only been dating for six months and I certainly was not thinking about marriage....so soon? It was not long after that when Kevin proposed to me and I said yes. We own and operate two businesses in Maryland, Night Flight Studio and Audio Assurance, where we assist churches with their sound systems.

The Jackson Family: Kevin, Sr., Stacy, Kayla, and Kevin, Jr.

Chapter 10

Walking into My Destiny

Each of us has a destiny that only we can fulfill. As I began to spend more time with God, continue to pray and read the Word of God, He began to show me there was more. I just kept hearing the word 'more.' God was not finished with me. A lot of times when you are a stay-at-home mom you tend to start to think: *Is this it for me? Is this all for me to do, raise my kids and be a wife and mother? Is that it?* I have two close friends, Sabrina Smith and Linda Parker, who are stay-at-home moms; we have had this same discussion. At times it seems like you do not have a life of your own, because your whole life is wrapped around your kids. For so long, it just seems that everything is about them. We take them places and oftentimes we put their needs before ours. We kind of put ourselves and our wants aside. But God revealed to me that there was more that He wanted me to do. I remember one of my pastors spoke these words to me, "Once your kids get older, God is going to use you."

In October 2009, we taped the show *"Unsung"* for TV One. When the show aired, it was as if God was saying, "This is not about you. This is about Me." Everything that I went through, every tear I cried, every dark place that I was in, God brought me out. He spoke these words to me, "This is a new season that I am calling you into. I am bringing you into a new season and people are going to see Me, not you." I remember years ago different people had prophesied that to me; and it is as if now it is beginning to take place. My friend Robyn Smith told me about Facebook. Because I have always been a very private person, I really was not in favor of having a Facebook page but I went ahead and got one. Now I see that God has been using it to prepare me for my ministry because I find myself ministering to people on Facebook all of the time. God used *"Unsung"* to give me a platform to begin to minister.

I am currently ministering at women's and youth conferences. I also speak in schools. One of my passions is to empower women, to let them know that God cares and that He loves them wherever they are in life. God's love is unconditional. Some things that we go through are not so much about us. As we go through them, we wonder if they will ever end. At times it seems overwhelming when you are going through something, but once you get to the other side where your victory is, you look back and realize that God was with you in the midst of it all.

Ministering the Word of God

It is so amazing how God uses the things that we go through. Our story equals God's glory. You can be a blessing to others by praying with them, encouraging them, and being a person of integrity. To me, long lasting blessings are when people can see your walk with God instead of your talk about God. These things have a lasting impact upon people's lives. Many people responded after the *"Unsung"* show had aired. I got over 200 messages from people on my Facebook page. Some of them said they were turning back to God after watching my story, "It was such an inspiration, such a blessing, that you stood for what was right. You didn't sell out. You didn't sell your soul."

The business part of the music industry is important to know. Having a good support system and a good manager and attorney are so very important because the music industry can be very cut throat. When I took a stand and walked away the way I did, I chose God's will, not mine. I am still getting messages from people talking about *"Unsung"* and what I stood for. I did not know that many people watched that show. I was in a store not long ago and a girl came up to me with her hand over her mouth and she just started crying. I thought she was hurt or something. She said, "Girl your story on *"Unsung"* really blessed me." As she just stood there crying I responded, "It's okay, please don't cry because if you don't stop crying you are going to make me cry."

My mission is to tell young women that you do not have to take your clothes off to become successful. You do not have to sleep with the company executives to gain wealth and fame, because at the end of the day your integrity will speak for you. That to me is priceless. Of course, you can make a million dollars and be rich materially, but poor spiritually. So which of these would we rather have? I would rather be rich spiritually than materially, because having a rich spiritual life is priceless. Money cannot buy a relationship with God. Money cannot buy peace. Money cannot buy contentment. Money cannot buy those things. Only a relationship with Christ can bring real peace and lasting joy. Outside of a relationship with God, there is no peace. It doesn't matter if you have the biggest house that money can buy, without God you are nothing! I believe there is a hole in us that only God can fill.

I went to a school not long ago and spoke to the students about being a leader and not a follower. We lead by example. You do not try to be in the clique and do what you know you should not be doing just because your best friend may be doing it. Leaders take a stand for what is right and always tell the truth. Leaders try and make peace and keep it. Leaders respect themselves and others. Leaders show patience, discipline, and determination. And leaders never quit! There's an old saying that we will know people by the company they keep. So it is very important that we teach our children the importance of being a leader and not a follower.

I recently launched my new company, *Believers Building Bridges (BBC)*. The mission of BBC is to help others to reach their goals. We will be opening a music center where we plan to have conferences in which we will focus on three different programs. First we'll have the youth empowerment program. Second is the Arts program in which we will discuss the music business—the do's and don'ts. People tend to think that it is glamorous and all fun, but it is not what people always think it is. There is a lot to the music business. I just have a heart to help people who are aspiring to be in the music industry. I want to share my experience and help others reach their goals and dreams.

And finally, I have founded a women's ministry called *"Women Walking with Authority."* My mission for this ministry is to be a vessel of God, for Him to use me through the Holy Spirit to empower HIS women in all aspects of life by HIS grace. My goal is:

- To equip them spiritually, emotionally, physically, socially, and financially;

- To encourage women to step out in faith and be the spiritual warriors that GOD has called them to be;

- To encourage and teach them to be women of integrity, reaching their goals and the desires of their hearts not by seeking the hand of GOD but the face of GOD;

- To spiritually equip them to be women of prayer and servants of GOD;

- To teach them how to acquire assets and ownerships of businesses in order to leave legacies for generations to come; and

- To teach them the importance of love, and the way GOD loves—unconditionally!

Within every human heart lies a hunger for significance. Therefore, we must know who we are in Christ and the authority that we have been given. Hosea 4:6 says, *"My people are destroyed for lack of knowledge."* So many times we tend to want to quit and give up, but we cannot give up because of the One who lives inside of us. The Bible says, *"Greater is He that is in you than he that is in the world"* (1 John 4:4). So we cannot quit. Winners never quit. We must also press— press forward and endure. Matthew 10:31 says, *"Fear not, then; you are of more value than many sparrows."* God sees great value and unlimited potential in all of us. When we learn to see ourselves as God sees us—victorious—our thinking will change, our minds will change and our lives will change. *As a man thinketh in his heart so is he* (Proverbs 23:7). The enemy will try and make us think we are worthless, but the truth is we are significant not for what we can accomplish on our own, but because of what Christ can do through us. And many times, He's just looking for a yes from us.

I got a message the other day from a lady who had just been diagnosed with cancer. It really touched my heart. I told her to stand on the Word of God. I shared with her different Scriptures on healing and told her to begin to confess them out of her mouth everyday and believe God for the manifestation of her healing. The Bible says that we **were** healed. It does not say that we were going to be healed, it says we were healed; that Jesus was wounded for our transgression and He was bruised for our iniquities (Isaiah 53:5). Not long ago, a man sent me a message on Facebook and told me that he was diabetic and was having problems seeing. He asked me if I would pray in agreement with him that God would fix his vision. I sent him some Scriptures on healing and he replied back and said that his eyesight was improving. I bless the Lord! That is what brings me joy.

A young lady sent me a message asking me to pray in agreement with her. She was broken and felt like giving up. I asked her to give me her number so I could call her. I called her and we began to pray. I said, "Let's pray and believe God. We are going to trust and believe Him." A few weeks later she sent me a message that said, "I just want to let you know God showed up and He answered

my prayer. I want to thank you for praying with
me." Some people say, "I am praying for you."
But do they really pray for you? I believe minis-
ters should be available if possible to pray with
and for others. God placed two pillars in my life
many years ago, Pastor Shirley Jones and Pastor
Irma McKnight. They are true women of God and
they have always been there for me. They pastor
a church, Rehoboth Family Life Center, in Upper
Marlboro, Maryland. I experience the presence of
the Lord each time I go there and I receive an on
time Word from the Living God. Halleluiah!

When we make ourselves available, whether
it's praying for someone or just doing a good deed,
God honors that because we are to be selfless not
selfish. The Bible says that the shepherd leads
the people. I like it when preachers take a few
minutes of their time after the sermon is over to
give people a handshake and a smile. Something
so small like that can make their day. Many times
they just want to know that the pastor cares and
has a connection with them. That is what some
people want, a connection with their pastor. I know
there is no way you can minister to a thousand
people personally, but I think it is good if you can
greet some of them. The church that we attend
in Gaithersburg, Maryland, has a large congrega-

tion, but our pastor, Pastor Dale O'Shields, is a fine example of what I'm talking about. He makes people feel welcome and appreciated. After the service is over, he is the first person at the door and he greets everyone as they leave the church. It really means a lot to have your pastor say hello, have a blessed day. It pleases God when we deny ourselves and make time for others.

I recall several times years ago when my husband was out of town, my pastor at that time, Pastor James Robinson, was always there for us. When Kev was 9 years old, he fell off his bike and hit his head on the cement. The knot on his head really frightened me. All I could do was pray. I rushed him to the hospital and called Pastor Robinson. He met me at the hospital; and another time when Kayla was sick, he was there for me. He got out of his bed in the middle of the night and met me at the hospital. Now that to me is being a servant, even when you don't feel like it. That is the heart of God. A servant has no agenda or will of his own; a servant follows behind God. Jesus was obedient even unto death; so a servant follows God and he does what God says to do and he says what God tells him to say. That is my heart. I want to be a servant of God, where people do not see me per se, but they see God; they see that I represent Him. We represent Him in the way that we dress. I always tell my kids that we represent God with what we wear; what we put on shows what type of person we are. When I see young ladies wearing clothes that reveal too much of their body, it's very degrading. And what type of men are you really attracting?

Integrity means so much to God. One of my prayers everyday is Lord let my life be an example of who You are. I want to be more like You. I pray every day that I may decrease that the Lord may increase in me. We are to be His hands, His mouthpiece, and His feet. Because with some people, we are going to win them over, not by what we say, but by the way we live, when we walk the walk and not only be a hearer of the Word but a doer of the Word. When we walk in love we are walking like Christ, because that is who He is. Love is the first fruit of the Sprit.

It is so important, even now, with the state of the world and the economy. If we can begin to love more, the world would be a better place. I live to please God not man. He will give you favor with man when you live your life to please Him. We all like nice things and God wants us to have nice things, but the Bible says, *"Seek ye first the Kingdom of God and all His righteousness and all these things shall be added unto thee"* (Matthew 6:33). Added, added! It is a by-product of righteousness. God supplies all of our needs and He also gives us the desires of our heart. The Bible says, *"Delight yourself in the Lord and He will give us the desires of your heart"* (Psalm 37:4), but many times we forget the first part of that verse. It says, *"Delight yourself in the Lord **and** He will give you the desires of your heart;"* so we must delight ourselves in Him first so that He can give us the desires of our heart. Oh glory to God!

Now getting back to that word 'destiny.' We all have a destiny. No one can fulfill or stop your destiny but you. I really believe that I am walking into mine. For many years I felt out of place. I did not know who I was. The truth is when you find out who HE is, HE'LL show you who you are! The Bible says that we are more than conquerors; we are the head and not the tail, so if we do not know who we are, we can be defeated. It is important that we find out who God says we are instead of who the world says we are. What the world says we cannot do God says we can do. The Bible says, *"I can do all things through Christ who strengthens me"* (Philippians 4:13). He did not say some things; He said all things through Him who strengthens us. I bless God for His faithfulness,

His keeping power, and His sustaining grace. The Bible says that He gives us brand new mercies every day (Lamentations 3:23). Before I step out of my bed every morning, I say, "Good morning God the Father, Holy Spirit and Jesus." That is just my way of acknowledging Him, of telling Him how much I appreciate Him for keeping me and sustaining me. God loves when we acknowledge Him.

It is just amazing when you learn to live your life for Him and not be so concerned about what people say about you. For so long, I was concerned about what people thought about me and said about me, when I walked away from the music business, but God had to deliver me from myself. My flesh had to die! That happens a lot with us. We must be delivered from ourselves first. So He had to set me free from myself, because I was too concerned about what people thought about me. I am a new person now, because the pride thing has been squashed. I can go to Walmart or any other store I want to shop at because other people's opinions no longer have a hold on me. I've been set free! I just want to please the Father. All that really matters is God being pleased with us—the way we live, the things we say, and the way we act, because we are to represent the Lord of Lords and the King of Kings. Halleluiah! And we are to let our light shine. If we are not doing our part, some people who do not go to church may never know Christ. They may never become born again. So if we live a life that pleases God, we can draw people unto Him by our lifestyles.

That is where I am today. I am renewed and walking into my destiny. I am doing what God has called me to do. I am yielded and willing; and I say yes and Amen.

I am not the same girl. I am renewed and walking into my destiny: *Therefore if any man be in Christ, he is a new creature: old things are passed away; behold, all things are become new* (2 Corinthians 5:17).

Experience New Life

in Jesus Christ

Have you ever wondered what your purpose is? Are you searching for meaning or direction? Are you restless or feeling like something is missing from your life? If you answered yes to any of these questions, you can begin to experience the beginning of a new life. I invite you to salvation in Jesus Christ.

Pray this prayer:

> Dear Heavenly Father,
>
> I acknowledge to you that I am a sinner and I ask for your forgiveness. I believe Jesus is the son of God and that He died for me and rose again on the third day. As I give my life to You, please transform my life so

that I may bring glory and honor to You. Right now I confess Jesus as my Lord and Savior....
Amen!

Welcome to the body of Christ! If you don't have a church home, pray and ask God to show you which church HE wants you to attend. There are books that inform, but only one Book that transforms—the Bible, the Word of God! God bless you as you begin your new life in HIM!

If you would like to receive more information or need reading material to help you with your new life in Christ, write to us or call (301) 292-9010.

Contact Information

Stacy Lattisaw Jackson is available to minister in word or song. For bookings, she can be reached at:

Believers Building Bridges
P.O. Box 44330
Fort Washington, MD 20749
(301)485-8507
Fax: (301)567-8413

stacy@stacylattisaw.net

www.stacylattisaw.net

CPSIA information can be obtained at www.ICGtesting.com
Printed in the USA
BVOW061703230412

288403BV00007B/1/P